POEMOGRAPHS

FOR

PEACE

a photo & poetry anthology

Cathy Warner, Editor

DEDICATION

For the contributors to this anthology
who offer their words as gifts.
And for all those who create
something of beauty
as we make meaning out of life.
Together may our efforts sing
a sliver of hope and healing into being.

CONTENTS

INTRODUCTION

Poemographs for Peace began as a community poetry project. From September 2021 through March 2022, I emailed a weekly photo as a writing prompt to a wonderful and widespread group of poets who shared their responses with one another in a private Facebook group. I emailed the photo without any explanation, and it was a delight to see the many ways in which an image can inspire a poem or remembrance. Some wildly divergent. Some very similar.

When April, which is National Poetry Month, came around I wanted to send a daily prompt, as has been my practice. I was also feeling the weight of unprovoked violence in the world, and I believe art and creativity can offer hope and new ways of thinking in response to the bad news that bombards us. So, this year, I asked recipients of the prompts to contribute to a charity aiding the people of Ukraine as I offered the prompts. Most had already made contributions to charities reflecting their interests and connections including: The Red Cross, The United Methodist Committee on Relief (UMCOR), Yoga International, DrumStrong, International Rescue Committee, Media Lifeline, and direct aid to a teacher housing refugee families. No wonder these poets inspire me.

Along with a daily photo in April, I wrote a three-line poem, in the spirit of haiku (or senryu which focuses on human nature rather than the natural world). Several poets responded with three-line poems of their own, and you'll find many of them in these pages, along with other fine poems from the weekly and daily prompts.

It is a gift to me to curate these poems and offer them to you, our reader. All royalties from the sale of *Poemographs for Peace* will be donated to the Ukraine aid projects of World Central Kitchen and UMCOR, where 100% of donations are passed on without administrative fees. I hope you'll help us spread the word and buy a copy for a poetry-loving friend!

Cathy Warner
Union, Washington
August 21, 2022

THREE FEET

BECAUSE

because the road
we walk is rocky
because life can be scary
because there is only one place
the path ends for all of us

we ought to walk
into the unknown
together and love
ought to be

the only pavement
beneath our feet
steadying every step we take

~ Cathy Warner

BEFORE HEAT

high summer
I rise
before the sun
shrug my way
into walking clothes
dress my feet sturdily
even in the dark
humidity presses
bitey bugs hum
I round the last curve
dawn breaks fully
I duck inside
before
the air
begins
to simmer

~ Lynn Oatman

STUCK IN THE MIDDLE WITH YOU

i didn't get the memo
that it was blue shoe day
i was always the odd one out
since i was little
head in the clouds
i missed a lot
of earthly rules
and mores
that helped others
to fit in
i was the square peg
always trying to catch up
feeling left out
because i didn't know
the importance and simplicity
of following the group
i wasn't conscious enough
or reckless enough
to stand out purposefully
i just backed into
being different
because i was unaware
of the supposed-to's
then, embarrassed
as if awakening
to find i was naked
in the midst
of a crowd
all in uniform
now,
i like my red shoes
and am unashamed

to wear them
while others opt for blue
who really cares, anyway
i take my cues
from my inner whims
not society's demands
finally free
of the me who wants
to fit the norm
finally free to me be

~ Gayle Lindsey Slaten

CANNED PEACHES

AMRITA

a cliché
to say they
taste like summer
warm and sweet
welcome any time
toothsome
flesh now
skinned and
quartered
packed into glass
for later consumption
do they dream
of sun that once
shown on them
as they ripened
hard green
to luscious yellow
amrita confection

~ Lynn Oatman

CANNED PEACHES

Into my dream marches
A brigade of love-canned peaches.
What waits behind?
What sweetness to foretell?

~ Dawna Peterson

RITUALS OF THE EQUINOX

Summer's essence
Encased in glass
Saved for savoring
In winter's waning light.
Anticipation sparks sensory
Memories of sunny orchards,
Sticky juices dripping from my chin,
Steamy kitchens,
Clove studded peaches,
Shared laughter with my aunt.
Together bid a rueful farewell to summer
While growing impatient
For autumnal family feasts.

~ Carolyn Wiley

SLICES

The Reaper's hands
Drip thick with syrup
From the sugars clinging
Seeping into my pores;
I am becoming those slices
Of fruit

Baskets have been collected
For preserves, jams, and butters,
A dessert wine
If I am lucky

The overspent skins
Now leathered and spent;
The remnants left
After the ravages of ant
Squirrel, deer, field mouse, tree rat and wasps
Had their way with the fallen meat

Colanders brim with freshly washed fruit
All pregnant with deliciousness
I am puckering
As I sink my teeth into flesh
Reminding me of the distinction
Between pleasure and pain
And how sometimes they are hard to distinguish

Soon apple butter
Will be drizzled on
My son's finely crafted pastries
Warming Pacific Northwest mornings
Reminding him
Of our two-tree orchard
The symbol of he and me;
The preciousness of childhood
Coupled with images
Of pancake art, soft flannel pjs

And frosty windows
Under a threshold of love

~ Michal Lauren

PEACEFUL PEACHES

I woke with a sense of peacefulness
Fading image of canned peaches
Homemade, sitting on a shelf
It gave me a sense of belonging
Being loved
Being worth the effort of
Picking, peeling, cutting
Beautiful, unblemished
Fully ripe peaches
Making the syrup
Sanitizing the jars
Canning the fruit I craved
Just for me
Warms my heart
I miss you, Grandma

~ Gayle Lindsay Slaten

PRESERVES

One simmering summer day
spent inside an orchard
on the outskirts of Yuba City
two sisters and their mother
with bandana-ed brows and bare hands
shimmied up ladders.
They picked perfect plump peaches
placed fuzzy-fleshed fruits
by fistfuls into canvas carriers
slung over shoulders as
the sun tanned their outstretched arms.
Sweat slicked the smalls of their backs
and laughter lilted from their lips
for what seemed like the first time
since the stepfather-slash-second husband
slunk away from his secondhand family
and left them to gather anything
within reach, which this day
tasted of high spirits and rare happiness.
Many decades later yellow fruit
glinting from a gleaming glass jar
becomes the very portal
to memories perfectly preserved.

~ Cathy Warner

CANNED STONE FRUITS

particularly peaches
most noble stone fruit
ripened in orchard summer
Central Texas hills
sap-smeared tumbled
bushels now purified plunged
exquisite fuzz and all
in boiling water till the slipping point
to be undone of skins
dipped in cold
while Mason jars heat
and sugar dissolves
to smother luscious fleshes
cut in quarters pitted
or as some put it
stoned
and now put by
suspended
nectar-wetted cheating time
till next time
on ice cream

~ Geoffrey Hall

CANADA GEESE

FLYING GEESE

A trio in flight
Above me
Concert of beauty

~ Dawna Peterson

THREE CANADA GEESE

Three came to the sand spit
Then three more,
Joyful greetings shared.
Six more joined in
Travel plans made.
Another nine
Circled in line
And took their place
Along the shore
And were joined
By eight more.
A rest, a feast, a festival.
The growing gaggle
Welcomed all.
Foray flights rise,
Circle and return,
Until one day
Farewell is said.
Silhouetted by the rising sun
They rise, circle, gaining height,
In V-formation they take flight
Like tourists on a holiday.
They tell the young
Of scenic sights
But shield them from
The perils ahead.
Adieu, warm weather friends
Adieu.

~ Carolyn Wiley

HONK!

Honk! said the geese in the open skyway.
Honk! Honk! was their cry as they flew over the bay.
Summer sun awaits them as they fly south to tan,
then home once more to Canada when the snow melts again.

~ Linda Whaley

Flying free, flying far
we can't say for sure where we are
but near and here—enough.

~ Carol Park

EARTH ANGELS

I fly with my earth angels:
My partner and son.
They flank me
Holding me up
When I forget
I have wings
Reminding me
I am strong.
I have focus
And direction.
Love and tenderness
Are always the answer.
Life is good
With my earth angels.

~ Gayle Lindsay Slaten

GUEST COTTAGE

I SIT WITH LIGHT

I gaze out to the morning light
wondering how to put my thoughts into words you'll understand
I sit with the Light of Understanding

I behold the passing clouds
pondering how they move effortlessly across the morning sky
I sit with the Light of Illumination

I take in the flower's cobalt blue
wondering how you infuse our world with ecstasy and ease
I sit with the Light of Inspiration

I imprint on my mind the sun's creep along my breakfast table
reminding myself that there is no darkness that cannot be dispelled
by Light
I sit with the Light of Remembering

And drink my tea bathed in your Holy, Holy Light

~ Lisa Sadleir-Hart

INSIDE / OUTSIDE THE FRAME

I had scrawled lines between lines
when I looked outside the frame of the page
to see through a rectangular window frame
Deep blue flowers inside
light blue waters, skies outside.
Earth brown wooden table inside
brown earth garden outside.
I decided not to write.
I stepped into the clouds.

~ Thom Woodruff

POINT ROBERTS

Such is the longing
To return to the hand-hewn cabin
That sits on the tip of Point Roberts
On the very edge of Puget Sound.
Precariously poised on pilings
Where it has stood for more
Than a century
Despite the poundings
By the unpredictable force
In the repeating sets of swells.
Pulled at by ever-churning tides
Defying gravity
This magical place
Remains where fresh
And saltwater commingle.
The ridge beam has bowed
To the weight of wet.
The unstable foundation
Alludes to a verse in Matthew.
How fitting it might be
For a writer such as I
To be taken down
In the inevitable wreckage
Whilst flooding thoughts are drowned
And my last recitation
Becomes lost in an estuary
Of submerged prose.
My final prayer being:
To become One
With the resounding elements.
To be set free. Eventually.

~ Michal Lauren

WAITING

If you wait for inspiration to write you're not a writer, you're a waiter. —Dan Poynter

I will write today
But I'm waiting
For my muse to
Bring blessed inspiration.
The scene is set
The pencil waits
Upon unsullied pages.
The coffee cools.
The sun drifts southward
Casting oblique shadows
Across the waiting table.
The last larkspur stems
Sit silently waiting
To offer insights
On garden growth
And summer's end.
Outside snowless
Blue mountains wait
For icy rains to dust
Sharp ridges with new snow.
A breeze ruffles dry grasses
And stirs turning leaves.
Writing can wait.
Inspiration draws me outdoors.
I'll write another day
'Cause I'm no writer
I'm a waiter.

~ Carolyn Wiley

PUMPKIN PATCH

PUMPKINS, JACK

Most are strangers to each other
undone, displaying trauma stumps
severed from sprawling family networks,
removed from sweet home turf.

Kids point at the orange rumble-tumble
nearly covering the quaint courtyard
church drive for hard-luck humans' benefit,
priced too high for passers-by

till one or another becomes enriched
with urge to stab, scalp, gouge.

~ Geoffrey Hall

TWISTED CHUNKIN' AUXILIARY
Dedicated to all "pumpkin chunkin" participants

Pumpkin after pumpkin tossed in bins
strewn on sawdust waiting for fingers
to clutch them by gnarly handles, evaluate
their grotesque merits—seek an ideal
gargoyle, knucklehead, or goose bump gourd
to disembowel, carve into award-winning jack-o'-lanterns
while sharing twisted versions of *Cinderella*,
the *Wizard of Oz*, and *Legend of Sleepy Hollow*.

Ancestral souls called between dusk & dawn
Ichabod Crane's exploits enthralled
while tales of anti-heroes & sheroes who
took the fall for friends, lovers & Hessian
auxiliaries inspired us to rummage
through each contorted patch selecting
bumpy, warty, blemished pumpkins
we'd sculpt into a hideous likeness

of the Headless Horseman's ghost rising
from his grave, seeking his missing skull,
allowing Debbie to focus her imagination
chiseling turnips, potatoes, and sugar beets
while the rest of us cut into orange flesh,
created frightening faces, fired inner candles,
placed handiworks on the porch to ward off evil spirits,
illuminated *Día de los Muertos* celebrations.

~ Sterling Warner

THE GOURD AT HARVEST TIME

My heart
Once full and round
Soft like the gourd at harvest time.
Autumn found the gleaner's hand.
Seed and guts scattered on the ground.
The shell of the calabash
Thin and spent.
The soul of the fruit
Lay fallow on a fertile bed.

In the whispers of spring's greening
New life aroused the vengeance
Of a lover's yearning.
My heart renewed
By the season's hope
Like a sacred chalice overflowing.
Pumpkin seeds sprouted
With tendrils striving
Round my stem
Leaves entwining.
Salutations dressed in green.
Life's longing to fulfill itself
Awakened.

~ Michal Lauren

PLUMPKINS

Orange orbs of pie delight.
Perfectly plump and sized just right.
Not too short and not too tall.
Round like the harvest moon in fall.
Filled with seeds and pumpkin goo
That makes us squirm and then shriek, "Ewwww!"
One to carve and set outside
and one to stuff our cheeks real wide.
Fall and pumpkins go hand in hand.
They stretch our smiles and our waistbands.

~ Linda Whaley

PUMPKINS

cut into a pumpkin
for a Halloween jack-o'-lantern
or a Thanksgiving pie
cut into a pumpkin
and autumn spills out
an overflow of summer
insides the color
of July and August sun
the shell a shade
of changing leaves

~ Lynn Oatman

ABANDONED HOUSE

EMPTY

completion achieved
residents gone
cars garaged
food shelved
dishes drained
evenings
sunset moved
across the vista
the house
empty
except for dust

~ Lynn Oatman

FEATHERS OF A FISH

The miraculous
shows itself
to the blind one,
dancing soundlessly.

Within the dark house
solitary
on the edge
of the forest, nothing
exists. The music
of dust.

Without, the field of weeds
is floodlit,
luminous, praying
to the moon.

Witness, you cannot
walk away from
this. Your mind will
carry it as a puzzle
to work
relentlessly
as you sleep.

~ Genet Bosque

RAISIN SCONES AND TEA

Grandma had a porch swing
where we'd swing and drink iced tea.
She put sliced lemons on the glass rim,
and baked raisin scones for me.
I'd watch Grandpa in the garden
tending to giant stalks of corn,
while Grandma stitched a shirt sleeve
Grandpa had accidentally torn.
When Grandpa spied us swinging,
he'd wave to us with glee
and join us on the back porch
for raisin scones and tea.

~ Linda Whaley

WHO LIVES HERE?

Who lives in the house by the side of the road?
It is not a new house but one with history.
Trees have marched down the steep hillside,
and now embrace the small clearing
with expansive views of mountain ridges beyond the estuary.
On the deck, a porch swing is carefully situated
to best catch the last splash of color from a sinking sun.

Grasses creep uphill from the road to buffer traffic's hum.
Encroachment by Mother Nature protects
the inhabitants of this peaceful citadel.

~ Carolyn Wiley

TO WHERE TWEEZLES (TEASELS) GROW

Take me to the place of thistle down
Where we would make wishes
On each airborne seed
We thought of as faeries.
Take me to where the tweezles grow,
In the open fields of autumnal gold.
Dried, the stiff-hooked bracs
Clung to my long hair when harvesting.
We would paint them silver and gold
Nesting the oversized barbs
To make wreaths and package decorations.
Such were childhood follies;
sweet memories of Grandma Jessie.
Cherished are the days of going to the country,
Far beyond the East Bay mud
To the joy of manifesting magic
Among the skeletons waiting in wanting pastures.
These remembrances of gaiety,
Are now my ways of daily being.
I am graced to be able to fall in love
Over, and over, with the sacredness of nature.

~ Michal Lauren

The house sits vacant
like my heart just waiting
for sweet reunion

~ Cathy Warner

BRONZE EAGLE

COLONY

We are a colony
you see three
but we are many
more than the
eye envisions or
brain perceives
murder one and
ten more leggy bodies
fill the void it left

~ Lynn Oatman

WEBS

I sing an ode to the Orb Weaver
that geometric genie extraordinaire
she swings to and fro with fever
spinning palaces from thin air

~ Cathy Warner

CATCH AS CATCH CAN

Sparkly dewdrops hung with care
on silky webbing a spider spun
to catch an eagle in mid-air
and show the world what can be done
with a vision bigger than just a wish,
or hopes that never come to be,
instead achieving with a flourish
a spectacular display of creativity.

~ Linda Whaley

BALD EAGLE

Webs spun over a hard and calculating
      eye of a black, iron-hard
         yard adornment.

White strings spun by one or countless eight-
      legged creatures—each line slim and
         flimsy—but together

they weave a robust net over the eagle's eye,
      where a gargantuan, malevolent
         spider seizes shelter.

The breeze coming off the Hood Canal does not
      rattle the hairy creature's hold nor
         the capture of the eagle's eye

the vision of democracy entrapped. Numerous threads concocted
      this tight web: media fabrications, power plays, and pig-
         headed, partisan ploys steal fair sight,

American Eagle rendered blind.

~ Carol Park

EAGLE STATUE WAKES

Feathers tarnished with inattention, flecked
with verdigris, American memory
nudges its beak between frame threads
of time's dew-wetted spiderweb life-
to-death boundary, ideas reduced to things:

human swarms, hypnotic architecture,
deadly crash-glass, wires, growly autos,
asphalt—wasteland—feral hogs
but not a blessed bluebird, let alone
a proper eagle, here to distant haze.

This hard-imagined ideal stands
For *country* where countryside once lay.
Did the sculptor leave no heirs? Or is this it?
It won't, In God We Trust
do the noble thing: topple and crush us.

~ Geoffrey Hall

INDRA'S WEB

Imagine a multidimensional spider's web in the early morning covered with dew drops, every dew drop contains the reflection of all the other dew drops, the reflections of all the other dew drops are in that reflection. And so, ad infinitum. That is the Buddhist conception of the universe in an image. ~ Alan Watts

Out of molten metal poured and cast
An eagle;
The quintessential symbol of Freedom is formed.
Wet, weathered, dripping in avian excreta.
It stands enshrouded in spiders' orbs.
Reminding me of Indra's Net.

I, like you
Live on an infinite web,
Interconnected,
Always reflected,
In every facet of self we choose to show
...And those we don't,
Reveal themselves, ultimately.
You may catch a glimpse of yourself in my glint.

Like the silk on this bronze bird
I am collecting wrinkles, scars, and stories.
My temples are gaining strength with their greying.
Some freedoms are born out of aging;
Such as an unbound knowing, a sense.
Some will choose to be stoic,
Rigid, like historic statues.

We are but a strand of pearls,
Growing more lustrous,
Shaped and layered with each experience.
We are tied together,
Knotted and bound,
In a shared humanity.

May these yarns I spin,
Capture the intricacy of emotions,
And the divine importance how feeling free,
Brings a lightness of being, an acceptance.

The Eagle;
A magnificent bird crafted with such power,
Is tethered.
Its weight alone has clipped its wings.
May we learn to loosen our tight grips
On our hearts, our minds, our souls,
So, that when we are called
And we become that longing
And embrace our lightness of being,
We may let go;
To be set free,
Of our human trappings,
And our illusions of power.

~ Michal Lauren

STAINED GLASS

This emptiness
does not feel itself
lacking.

Fractured colour—
lime papaya blueberry lemon
iridescence—lights the room

Holy: a God carnival
waiting
to begin.

~ Genet Bosque

CYBERNETIC CELEBRANT

Robotic humans fill hard oak pews
genuflect in unison, listen for bells
strike fists against hearts like programmed droids
while children gaze at stained glass windows
like picture books, attempting to decipher
Latin words scrawled above holy figures.
Halogen lights reveal altar dust balls
squirreled away like tabernacle nuts.
Jasmine incense drifts towards heaven
leaves misfit souls on their knees,
eyes ever upward, autumn cornucopia
of fallen maple leaves, diablo winds,
and fresh rain invigorating senses
overpowering deep pocket doldrums—
hazy Indian Summer's smoky vestiges.
The deacon preaches forgiveness
yet rails against excess self-indulgence
preparing for impending earthly gales
directing his flock to take comfort
in painful lives of good works, a sermon
as predictable as a prerecorded speech.

~ Sterling Warner

Even now, the promise
still appears in living color despite
all we have killed in his name.

~ Cathy Warner

NONE OF YOUR BUSINESS

What I believe
whether I believe
that's my business
mine alone

Mom laid down the law
insisted on Sunday school
until I was old enough
to question why
she did not attend

Don't pray over me or for me
I can fend for myself
and in my mind and heart
there are no casual conversations
about religion

If I sleep in on Sundays
tend to yourself

What I believe
is not for you
to question

~ Lynn Oatman

My Old Church

So straight,
so hard
such right angles
of old wooden pews.
Same too with stained
glass windows
with Jesus' body
so odd,
so elongated and
face so small.
No smile, no tears,
no care, no
reach of warmth.
Is this what pew sitters
know of my Jesus?
I hope also they see
light shining
through the host
of bright glass pieces.
May lime-green and
yellow splashes
on pews, on floors
pierce through
severity and stolidness.
May they know
more than right angles,
hard injunctions
grim harshness
so often—so
misspoken, from
stained pulpit to pews

~ Carol Park

MY FIRST CHRISTMAS

I was thirty-two.
A nice Jewish girl with her Italian beau.
My son, five, moved cross-country
With me. New adventure. New family.
Seven children in my beau's household,
All teens by then
Conspired to make my son's first Christmas
One to remember.
Suddenly, sleigh bells were heard on the roof.
My son, eyes as big as saucers,
Became a true believer.
Santa was real.
Off to midnight mass
He felt older, staying up
And sitting on the wooden benches
We were both in awe
Of the stained-glass windows
And of the friendly crowds
All turning to shake our hands.
When they asked heads of family to stand
I got up.
To my surprise, they handed out ornaments.
My first, which later went on a tree
We chopped down on our nine
Ann Arbor acres.
As we left the service,
Snow began to fall
Also a first
For this California transplant.
The perfect Christmas Eve.
And now that my son is a father
I wonder how he makes

Christmas magical
Remembering that moment
From long ago, giving
His children the gift
Of joy in the holiday season
To believe in Santa
Even if only for a while.

~ Gayle Lindsay Slaten

PROMISES

I saw a rainbow today
when I visited God at his house.
I remembered the story
where he told Noah
he wouldn't flood the earth again.
God said he would send a rainbow
to remind Noah of that.

Today it reminded me
that when the sky gets dark,
and the rain comes down,
and the power fails,
I don't have to worry
about the earth being flooded.
And if I don't have to worry
about something as big as that,
then I shouldn't worry
about other, smaller things either.

~ Linda Whaley

FIRST FROST

KNITTED CRYSTALS

We have been kissed again
By the bitter bite of cold.
It is the moment
That marks the distinctions
Between seasons.
Nature's primary colors of autumn
Are being swept,
Overcome by a determined
Browning carpet.
The skeletons of trees
Make for haunting shadows
That dance in the longer dark nights.
Tonight, the Beaver Moon
Will light the way

For burrowing critters
To take to their shelters
Under frosted blankets of knitted crystals

~ Michal Lauren

QUESTIONS TO A FROSTED LEAF

Draped over a bed of rocks
The frost ladened leaf catches my attention
and begs me to notice its life's end...

What is it like to coldly decay and return to earth?
What is it like to lose substance and give way to gravity?
What is it like to finally let go, yield, surrender
to this particular planetary coordinate?

Do you talk back to the frost as it covers the fiber of your being?
Or do you embrace the crystalline forms that rest gently
on your veins?
Do you shutter and balk at the inconvenience of being so cold?
Or do you shimmer and smile as the autumnal light
catches each crystal?

How is it that you came to be here?
How is it that you were released from the branch above?
How is it to die alone and underfoot?
How is it to go home?

~ Lisa Sadleir-Hart

LACE LEAVES

Today God painted icy lace
upon the crisp brown leaves
that were stacked upon the ground
at the bottom of the tree.
The wind whistled through the branches
where the leaves had once clung tight
before wafting slowly downward
bidding the tree a fond goodnight.
Leaf blankets tucked the tree in snugly
for its winter hibernation
and in decay sent nutrients
back to their final destination.
And in the spring the tree awakened
and stretched its branches wide
to make room for all the new leaves
that would come forth from inside.

~ Linda Whaley

FIRST FROST

The last visage of beauty lies
Coated in crystalline ice
The promise of spring
Lime green emerged
From winter's sleep
Flourished under
Summer's sun
Released in
A golden
Shower
That
Glowed
Before fading
To crisp sienna
Dried and drifted
To a lonely gravely
Grave arrayed in
Silver finery
Not death
Renewal

~ Carolyn Wiley

WOODSTOVE

Together we sweat
by the light of the fire.
Does the flame-licked heat
come from outside our bodies
or within?

~ Cathy Warner

MY OLD FLAME

Once
I turned to you for warmth.
I felt the heat of your passions.
Your fire spurred action in the face of injustice.
Your light overcame the darkness.
Today you move to a silent symphony.
Your dancing shadows climb the walls.
I am lulled to sleep
Beside your cooling embers.
You radiate love.
You are my old and only flame.
Though I know
Some time
There will be ashes,
I know
Our eternal flame
Lives on.

~ Carolyn Wiley

FIREWOOD

Daddy chopped the firewood
and stacked it up with care
so we could have a fire
when wintertime was here.
Momma sewed the quilts
and knitted winter socks
that kept us warm when winter storms
came whistling through the locks.
Then sister and I would make cocoa
and play checkers or card games
while Momma & Daddy snuggled on the couch
to watch the dancing fire flames.

~ Linda Whaley

ISINGLASS

I carry the vestiges of trees
That warm my hearth.

I have carried the burden of unresolved relations
That I no longer have the strength for.

Is it imagination or illusion?
I see an angel dancing behind the isinglass.

My attention is drawn
To the pyre like a moth

Thoughts fly
Like embers in a gust

Swirling emotions, and cinders burn
Worlds float in streams of consciousness.

I have struggled with betrayal,
Leaving me near death.

I am awakening
From an arduous journey of healing

Baby steps
As I brush off the ashes

While the Phoenix in my soul rises
Beyond my baptism in fire.

~ Michal Lauren

SUGAR, SUGAR

DEAR SMIDGE

Dear Smidge,
Oh Sugar, sugar, you poor granulated girl.
Don't you see that spilling yourself
with honeyed glances so cloying and sweet
and sticking to any silver spooned suitor
dissolving under any tongue
is unseemly when pure upright restraint
is what we require to be bought
and paid for?
It's time to shape up
or you'll linger on the shelves.
Sincerely,
Your C&H (Conservative &Holy) friends

~ Cathy Warner

WHEN SWEETNESS SPILLS

Sometimes,
The unthinkable happens
Crawling under our skin
Festering like a splinter
Until our ability to cope
Releases us,
Leaving an indelible scar that imprints.

Sugar is arduously made.
When mixed with water,
Dried, left to sheet,
and spilled outside its container,
Its shards can pierce like glass
And cut to our core.
An ache like a thousand paper cuts.

Unconscionable moments
Can throw us into a place of paralysis.
They wax and wane,
For the rest of our days.
Memories can slice into our hearts
Lingering just below
The surface of our skin
In the secreted places in our souls.

~ Michal Lauren

JIM-BOB, TOKELAND WA

WORKING ON SHIPS

Scraping the rust
I scraped myself
Back into service
Floated away...

~ Thom Woodruff

LIFE ON THE SEA, WILLAPA BAY

Home is the sailor, home from the sea, / And the hunter home from the hill.
"Requiem" ~ Robert Louis Stevenson

Moored, immobile
Restive idleness,
Safe harbor boredom
Pervades the marina.
Weather beaten,
Rusty hulks
Piled high with
Crab pots
Wait for the tide
To set them free
Upon the winter sea.
Beyond the jetty
Keels will be set toward
The coastal crabbing
Grounds in quest of
Dungeness, Red, or King
Commercial industry
Balanced on the brink
Questioning the
Recovery—or extinction
Survival or a brutal end
Of a livelihood and a species.
Still and silent harbors
May not mean safe.

~ Carolyn Wiley

RUSTY BILGE FIBONACCI

Green
lights
flash on
tides roll back
a blue moon rises
diesel engine sputtering as
Jim-Bob stacked empty
saltwater
traps and
fyke
nets

on
his
troller's
wooden hull;
towering over
the eight-foot standing shelter, gulls
patiently lurching
quite aware
piston
snaps
mean

meals:
packed
shrimp pots
that promise
fresh spills—food—as the
vessel slices perpetual
harbor oil slicks, bright
rainbow waves
crest on
its
wake

~ Sterling Warner

SEAWORTHY

Christened with two names
may the Jim-Bob
itself bob doubly buoyant
in treacherous swelling seas.
And may Jim-Bob's
catch be double-sized,
may its hold overflow
and prosper the lives
of captain and crew.
May its reach
ripple far into parts unknown.
Jim. Bob. Joined.
Twice named.
Twice blessed.

~ Cathy Warner

GREAT BLUE HERON

Caped conductor
lifts her arms to lead avian chorus
in haunting song
exposing salmon bike shorts.
She of many talents
always ready
for a quick escape.

~ Cathy Warner

THE RIVER DANCERS

The river dancers were dressed and ready for
The performance of their lives

Blue capes and orange tights, feathered necklaces
Gave them a sense of purpose, they were a team.

The leader stepped out first,
Posed as the others lined up
Like a conductor, he faced them, raised his cape in ready.

Together, they performed
For the water, sky, and land
Thanking their surroundings in a ritual
That was passed down through generations.

Showing their appreciation
For being welcomed into this scene,
Melding with nature's rhythm
They were home.

~ Gayle Lindsay Slaten

HONORING THE ANCESTORS

Arriving first,
The choirmaster waited patiently
While choristers drifted in
And assumed their rightful places
Along the shoreline smorgasbord.
Heads bowed in watchful contemplation
Until roused from idle isolation,
By the director's commanding pose.
Tone and pitch established,
Blended voices raised
In raucous inharmonic praise
The ancestral hymn's cacophony
Of the pterodactyl chorus
Begins.

~ Carolyn Wiley

THE DANCE

Forgoing its usual aggressive nature
a blue heron steps lively in shallow shores
of Annas Bay; fierce predator gone lover
beak held straight like an elegant monolith
neck stretched gracefully as the courtship
proceeds, extended digits touching sand–barely–
talon-like toes practically levitating while long legs
navigate the shallow water ever conscious of rites
the croaking wader calls out to all who will listen
& it erects azure plumes, majestically flagging wings
in slow motion–beckoning–vaunting its powder down
chest, flaunting its beauty, attracting a mate.

~ Sterling Warner

WINDOW CURTAINS

Weak winter sun summons
those cloistered behind glass and lace
with provocative promise

~ Cathy Warner

ONLY

What is open to us
beyond the glass we
enclose ourselves
behind — peering out
afraid to truly
venture?

Beyond the perfectly-placed
picnic table, the manicured
chartreuse lawn: only
the whole marvelous
unpredictable
uncontrollable realm of
Nature — the mercurial
elements, astonishing colours,
unforeseen weather and meetings
on the trail — the
danger and glory of
life fully lived. Only
everything that
quickens us
to the marrow.

~ Genet Bosque

BEHIND THE CURTAINS

It has become,
Behind the curtains that buffer me
From the present communal condition.
I am trying to avoid the precarious moats
Abundantly floating amongst us.
*

Aerosols are aggressively seeking to fill voids
In all the vulnerable recipients
On which to breed and spread.
It is as if this virus
Has a consciousness on whom to occupy.
This week; my son.
*

It is behind the lace
Where I create
In hopes that my acts of beauty
Will overcompensate for a world in grief.
It is as if we are in the hands
Of the multiheaded god Ravana*
Toying with all our unresolved karma.
*

With all these slaying thoughts of dis-ease,
I am trying to understand the partitions in this country.
Whilst the "want to be political celebrities"
Keeps the vision of democracy
In the sickening, and unconscionable clutches of privilege.
They overtly disregard science,
As they resurrect the oppression of Jim Crow.
*

The Iron Curtain, I tried to help melt,
With love from the voices of children singing songs
For the dream of a world that shares the vision of peace.

My Ukrainian friends are being preyed upon
By the tightening reigns of a malevolent war lord.
Who spews only vitriol.
*

I pray for the day
I open my curtains without tears in my eyes.
I am knitting woolen yokes of warmth to be worn as a kiss.
May each stitch in these cowls help mend,
The broken parts of the hearts of the wearer.
I will wrap myself in tenderness
To weave us together in the divine light of love.
*

Will you take my hand and walk with me,
Where freedom rings?
Somewhere,
Beyond the partisan blinds,
where puny men and women hide?

~ Michal Lauren

*Ravana (/ ˈrɑːvənə /; Sanskrit: रावण) was a king of the island Lanka and
the chief antagonist in the Hindu epic Ramayana and its adaptations.

INFINITE CLEARANCE

We arc and eclipse
in eternal ellipses
by the divine transfixed

~ Cathy Warner

INFINITE CLEARANCE

Infinity
Like Divinity
Goes on,
Forever and ever

Humanity's history
Is no deep dark mystery
But an endless trip
On a Möbius strip
Leading us
Back to our
Starting point
That savage
Experience
Renders unrecognizable.

Until the
Last breath
We exist in 3-D
With two sides
In every conflict
Traveling on
One edge
Continuing
Without end.

Flight of fancy
In search of
The infinite,
Cleared for
Take off.

~ Carolyn Wiley

MÖBIUS TRIP #2

Mesmerized
     By bigotry
          And hate
Some lives
     Are lived
          Locked into
An insular
     Journey on a
          Möbius strip.
Two sides
     One edge
          One centerline
Continuously
     Retraced
          A thousand times
Traveling through infinity
     On a march with no end
          And no known beginning
Circling nothingness
     Existing in space
          Absorbed in a limited life
Finding comfort
     In the closed circle
          Membership exclusive
Never opened to "other"
     Safely ensconced
          And unchallenged.

~ Carolyn Wiley

MÖBIUS STRIP

Stopped in my tracks
On this Möbius strip.
Making my way,
Neither under or over.
Tripping reluctantly
Into a questionable future,
Not knowing if I am above
Or below the horizon line.
As I embrace the gravity
Of the infinite mystery.

~ Michal Lauren

RIALTO BEACH

Down the log-strewn beach
walks my husband
who has weathered too many
storms to count.
Always I trail behind
learning from him
how best to navigate life.

~ Cathy Warner

HERRON ISLAND

The rocky beaches
Of Herron Island
Once called to me
Sometimes serene
Watching boaters
In the distance
I'd walk to the petrified logs
Sit down and meditate
Or look for tiny seashells
And uniquely colored stones along the shore

Other times
The sadness of seeing
A baby seal washed ashore
Or a dead deer
Which had run scared
Off the cliff above

A tire swing hung on a tree
Part way up the cliff
Enticing children
To test their bravery
While others watched
One time, a drunk adult
Walked the windy path
To the swing,
Fell onto the rocks below
And had to be rescued by water

When my adult children
Came to visit
This beach was a favorite adventure

Laughing, exploring
Talking with other residents
Of this tiny island paradise

I left long ago
But these memories linger
The draw of the beach
The view of islands
And sparkling water
Feeling nature's energy
Today, I am far from a beach,
Surrounded by saguaros and desert views
Happier here

~ Gayle Lindsay Slaten

ELEMENTAL EVIDENCE

1.
Not the first footprints on the wet sand
Nor the last below the high-tide line
Below the jumbled heaps of
Silvered logs and gnarled stumps
Newcomers arrive
Ocean-tossed tree trunks
Bark intact, but gouged and broken
Shattered trunks attest to the
Power of the wind and rain that
Weakened riverbanks
Landslides stripped roots
And smashed huge firs upon
The jagged rocks below
Amber orange splintered wood
Splayed like rays of light

Tossed atop ancient driftwood
A toddler's tantrum
Ripped from the earth
Cast into the raging river
Smashed and scraped
In a tumbling rush to the sea
Driven ashore to rest
Until the next winter king tide

2.
On the solitary shoreline
Nature's diary of destruction
Records the power of water.
Delivered by ocean currents
Fulsome storm clouds
Released tons of water
On rain-nurtured upland forests
Ravenous rivers gnaw
Into glacial riverbanks
Unstable land gives way
Forest duff, dirt,
Sand, pebbles, rocks
Boulders, and trees
Slide into roiling waters.
The weight of life now lies
Shattered at the tide line.
A testament to water's power
To create, nurture, divide,
Erode, uproot, and split asunder.

~ Carolyn Wiley

GIRAFFES

Double Take

That grinning face in the mirror is
just me, just me; I recognize the jawline
the man bun, the beard, yet regress
to my childhood surrounded
by stuffed animals, snuggling
with Audrey, my long-necked giraffe.

I've walked by this mirror before
caught reflections of my parents
in twisted positions, curling tongues
like Audrey as she munched down
on imaginary saplings, eyes locked
like a steamer trunk bound for exotica.

~ Sterling Warner

TRANSFORMED

(The transforming effect of gossip)

Small town
Cozy
Cafe
Shared time
Two friends
Transformed
Into
Gawking
Giraffes
Next booth
Fresh news
Is heard
Ears flare
Necks stretch
Eyes widen
"Did you
Hear that?"
"Did they
Just say?"
Bill paid
Tip laid
Small Town
Gossip
Spreads by
Giraffe
Gazette

~ Carolyn Wiley

TREE OF LIFE

Sitka Spruce, Kalaloch Beach, Olympic National Park

SUSPENDED

Barely hanging on between two cliffs of sand
How can I root now?
Where is my link to the source?
How will I continue to reach for the sky?
Where will the birds roost when I'm gone?

Mother Ocean, please help me release.
Mother Ocean, please cradle my soul.
Mother Ocean, I'm coming home.

~ Lisa Sadleir-Hart

WHAT WE SUSTAIN

Or has everything happened, / and we are standing now, quietly, in the new life?
—from "Oceans," Juan Ramon Jiménez

What we sustain
what we endure
suffer
come to accept

What we discern
what we comprehend
recognize
sense
distinguish

What we seize
what we possess
deduce
crave

What we
spring from
hustle to
trot on
whisk away

What shivers
splinters
penetrates
what digs
what deepens

What remains
what stays

what holds
what calls
what propels

What we swirl
what we simmer

What stands
what settles
what rests
unbends
slackens

We abide
we endure
we pause
we dwell
we breathe
everything

Oh, how we breathe
all of it

Into the now of
this life

~ Jan Haag

LOOK INTO THE VOID

A world to build, a world to destroy,
I can do nothing, I am only one,
One living cell
One drop of water,
One grain of sand
One human.
Each has the power to create or destroy.

Examine the void
There is nothing to see,
Nothing but the future.
Agents of change can be microscopic
And seem inconsequential, but
Natural forces assure inevitable change:
Living cells,
Drops of water,
Grains of sand,
Individual humans.

One seed germinates.
Cell by living cell
The seed becomes a mighty beacon.
Unseen, a wide intertwined network
Captures life giving moisture.
The force of transpiration columns moisture and minerals
To the highest boughs.
For ages the beacon fir
Stood watch at the rim of the bluff.

Untamed drops of water respond to gravity
Seep and trickle along roots
Loosen foundation soils.

Dislodged sand and pebbles
Crumbled and tumbled to the beach below
To be washed away by storm and tide.
Nurturing moisture
Becomes the means of destruction.

Outer fringe roots hold fast, sustain the still living cells
Of the giant suspended above the void.
Silent testament to;
The power of a living cell
The power of a grain of sand
The power of a drop of water
The power of a single human
The power of one cannot be discounted.
In the vortex of the void
The power of one becomes
The surging power of many.

~ Carolyn Wiley

Roots curved, tangled, fixed
in hollow 'tween two sandstone
cliffs—they hold up much.

~ Carol Park

THE TREE OF LIFE

Suspended in air
the giant Sitka spruce straddles
two sandstone cliffs defying
gravity and erosion.
Its canopy green
despite the lack of soil.
One can walk into the small
cave beneath this impossible
evergreen and gaze up
at the intricate network of roots
drawing sustenance
from nearly nothing and understand
that like this tree
it is our nature
to cling to life despite everything

~ Cathy Warner

SWORD FERNS

fiddleheads unfurl
as spring fern fronds emerge
sunlight coaxing growth

~ Sterling Warner

SNAIL

I do not see my ooze as troublesome,
nor the fact that my diet consists
of these tasty new stems and leaves.

Do you not see the loveliness
in the laciness of the green? It takes
hours to nibble such intricate brocade

into growing things—not destroying
them, but adding filigree, the most
delicate applique to nature's

exquisite decorations. The ones
you've waited all winter for,
anticipating their return,

to encourage and admire.

~ Jan Haag

RAILROAD TRACKS

We are parallel rails
We meet at infinity
Held to this rock earth
Until zen.

~ Thom Woodruff

STOWAWAYS

An Homage to The Canadian Railway Trilogy

Hangin' our heads like Gordon Lightfoot
Lange & I sang songs about navvies who worked
the railways hammering spikes, laying down
iron tracks, pinning them to dirt & gravel
scarring nature's pristine face east coast to west.

We studied the Capitola station agent
three weeks, noting when he threw the turnout
his habit of drinking a fifth of rot gut whiskey
once the noon train rolled on by & he completed
a daily crossword puzzle nonstop: hazy & content.

Hopping the empty Salinas crawler
cold rolled steel began taking on sparks, sliding
angrily beneath wheels—metal upon metal—
sleepers resting on ballast, absorbing vibrations,
like a weathered linemen morning, noon, & night.

Clandestine travelers, we reached a redwood grove
& abandoned our escapade with pocket watch precision
& punctuality, imagining gunpowder blasts removing boulders,
leveling the grade, picks & axes burrowing through mountains,
creating train tunnels so deep pitch engulfed light's façade.

~ Sterling Warner

FALLING

Pyramid Hill Sculpture Park, Hamilton Ohio

Okay! You got me!
Take your photo. Have your laugh.
April fool am I.

~ Dawn Smart

THE ART OF FALLING ISN'T HARD TO MASTER

Just starve between two haystacks like any jackass.
Or fall between philosophies, habits, laws.
Find yourself dispossessed, debunked
Like any old conspiracy theory.
Begin with one (or zero if Arabian).
Move into bipolar duets, or sing with orchestras.
Falling requires release to gravity
To just let go. To be. And, when you fall—
To feel release from all that holds you at all.
The art is in the falling... So—just fall.

~ Thom Woodruff

Foolish, fragile fear
Disperse! Recede! Evaporate!
Be gone! Love rules now!

~ Lisa Sadleir-Hart

TOUCHSTONE'S CROWN

Like Quasimodo, King of Fools,
beggars regard me as a lucky totem
& applaud my squirrelish behavior,
jingling orbs hanging off dangling
sleeve tips on a cap less oval than conical,
I knock over ashtrays & tea serving sets
while limping through antique shops
searching gifts of universal appeal

to every backyard, bench braking
Esmerelda sunbathing on my block

or through fancy imagined climbing
redwood slat fences, legs straddling
the post cap & swaying in the wind
like Norte Dame's cathedral bells
chimed into action, tintinnabulation

booming, oscillatory motions rocking
back & forth, side by side, to & fro.

Cheers to jesters & April first superstitions
that fuel creativity, abandon caution,
release from the best & worst traditional
daring that encourage carte blanche
comportment, hugging inky corners,
living to love, breeding peacemakers
in haylofts, snapping chains, replacing
numbing restraint in uninhibited motely.

~ Sterling Warner

April's holy fool
knows failure and bruises
Still she leaps, laughs, loves

~ Cathy Warner

APRIL FOOLS

Two fools
In love.
Went public
Broke the news
One April first

With josh
And nudge
And winking nod.
Kith and kin
Assumed the worst.

The joke's on you
My dear ones.
These April fools
Are celebrating
Sixty-plus years
Together.

Our love-bubble did not burst.

~ Carolyn Wiley

AIRPORT

Over Maritimes

we taxied forever
Ontario
grew closer and
I wondered if
perhaps we
were going to
have a bath
instead of
a flight but

liftoff was
successful and
we soared
over the lake
to the river
connecting Toronto
with the Atlantic

~ Lynn Oatman

SeaTac Tarmac

Queued-up planes filled with air rage passengers
stack like autos on I-5 during rush hour,

departing and arrival flights contesting space
while illuminated orange sticks direct traffic.

Alaska Airlines flight 69 taxis down
runway 16C; strapped-in attendants read

dogeared pages from Harlequin romance novels.
As wings lift the cabin heading east, pilots

set controls for Manhattan, even though
Broadway's now dead, and the city

often sleeps. Pushing pillows under heads
we set aside all differences, petty opinions,

imagine bare Boeing walls decorated
with redwood burl clocks, ticking, ticking,

ticking, keeping time past and present,
collecting cobwebs—silken highways—

enhancing conifer art, presenting overhead
bins with dignity, distinction, decorum.

~ Sterling Warner

TENORS

The Texas Tenors, Skookum Creek Event Center, Shelton Washington

Touring tenors
serenade silver-haired seniors.
Long live golden oldies.

~ Cathy Warner

Sing along with me
All trying for the same key
It's no mystery

~ Dawn Smart

R & R Silver Foxes

For Chuck Berry

Holding transistor radios to our ears, we
shuffled like James Brown, sang along
with the Beach Boys, embraced Motown magic,
hopped on board the British Invasion & imagined
reversing roles—listeners to practitioners.

Before brushing shoulders with rock stars backstage—
proud roadies setting up amplifiers gig after gig—
we sat on the Avalon Ballroom floor, our svelte
young bodies pressed against vibrating Vox speakers
booming so loud, they blew out our eardrums.

Young Turks to silver foxes, our own band evolved
while we aged barely noticing tight bellies growing
soft, uncut hair falling, smokestack lightening fingers
becoming arthritic; oh, curtains still fell, spotlights lowered
& sleeper busses rolled under reunited octogenarians.

A cavalcade of colors glanced over wizened faces
whispering half-forgotten lyrics through Shure
cardioid dynamic microphones, background singers
belting away lyrics our memories couldn't recall
stuck notes & bent lyrics like gymnasts on rosin.

Severe balding heads now wore hats as we embarked
on yet another final tour, many sons & daughters
filled-in for group fathers and mothers long since passed;
though blue beams retouched wrinkles, they're no substitute
for psychedelia, liquid slide shows, or single strobe encores.

~ Sterling Warner

TUG

The tug ran aground in Neva Strait
spilling oil, slicks of toxins cover
the surface of the deceptive blue waters.
How will we lay down our hemlock branches now?
Will the herring know it's not safe for them here?
When will we learn dear Mother?
When will we learn?

~ Lisa Sadleir-Hart

PUSH AND PULL

we are called
tugboats
but more often
we push
guiding loads
both empty
and full
through
a busy harbor

~ Lynn Oatman

MANEUVERS

Tug
boat
Annie
pulls empty
barges North towards
gravel pits, looking to haul
floating log rafts past
Seattle's
Salish
Sea
and
Sound

~ Sterling Warner

Sailing out to sea
emptied of all efforts
a companion guides the way

~ Cathy Warner

TACOMA NARROWS BRIDGE

WHILE THERE IS SPACE TO WALK

No pedestrians. Emptiness.
Lines of fast cars rush past.
They have no arrows...

~ Thom Woodruff

Head west this new morn
Straight ahead is the future
Unknown adventure

~ Dawn Smart

DIRECTION

This way,
the arrow points,
in case we are too
dim or dulled by
all the hubbub—

caught up in the fray
and traffic in our
minds and hearts
to discern the direction
we are meant
to travel—

forward, across
the span, into
the blue, always
looking ahead.

~ Jan Haag

TWIN SUSPENSIONS

Remembering Galloping Gertie

My stiff back cries out for compassionate
masseur fingers kneading, tapping, rubbing,
shaking my torso; both eyes on the road,
I swerve around motorists whose pent-up
road rage suggests they need spinal alignment
at alarming degrees as they weave between lanes,
advancing by inches that endanger & collide
into vehicles filled with workers & families:
radios mute, laughter ceases, chaos rules.

I jump through doors on my SUV, abandon
my car, stretch legs that'd pressed gas pedals
too many hours, days & years; my feet hit
hard asphalt liberating numbness & cramps
as I walked past pile-ups where victims
sought attention from ambulances & police,
crossed over twin Tacoma Narrows bridges
traveling west—walkway protected by a cement
barrier—& marveled at cable suspensions above.

Rising from the ashes of "Galloping Gertie"
the dual South Puget Sound crossings exposed
scenic vistas seldom observed by those steering wheels,
viewing the Olympic Mountains & Mt. Rainer
in the distance, watching boats slice water below;
the present State Route 16 ghost town is a momentary
reprieve before drivers resume passing at a snail's pace
or racing like contestants at the Indy 500 so, I return
to the blacktop jungle & long for deep tissue pressure.

~ Sterling Warner

There's no mistaking the bridge
from me to you the path from here
to there to somewhere together

~ Cathy Warner

Cerulean sky
Arrow points to You alone
I'm on my way now

~ Lisa Sadleir-Hart

WOMAN OF STEEL

Westport Winery, Washington

ROBOT WOMAN

Metal Warrior
How you shine!
Brighter than painted rust
Dust cannot stop your movements
Your dance Shiva/Kali
Earth itself...

~ Thom Woodruff

Stand tall you goddess
Go forth to vanquish evil
Conquer the despot

~ Dawn Smart

Rising up, I sing out
Calls for justice and mercy
Rising up, I am strong

~ Lisa Sadleir-Hart

Poseidon's daughter
pledges her power
to protect not pillage.

~ Cathy Warner

SEA GODDESS

Sea goddess, you are known on each shore by differing names,
Your powers defined and honored through cultural lore.
Ruler of winds, storms, and tides, you exist beneath frozen floes.
You float through tropic corals and swim
the canyoned unknowable depths.
Mother of crab and squid, dolphin and urchin, whale and krill.
Goddess, you taught us to live with the treachery of your wrath.
Goddess, you taught us to harvest the bounty of seasonal currents.
Sea goddess, you break the mirrored surface
to accept our adoration and praise.

~ Carolyn Wiley

RECKONINGS: IN MEDIAS RES

Long haired Achaeans let billows fill sails
to punish ignoble horse-taming Trojans;

listen to wind gusts whisper though
interlinked rings on the Greek cuirass;

steel strips hang like leather war
skirts covering thighs, deflecting blows

& verbal assaults—high battlefield fashion
where helmets, gauntlets & bracers

lay cast among those fallen as well as
living demi-gods repelling assaults

unwilling to renew onslaughts burning
ships moored on Ilium's beaches. Waiting—

waiting to emulate Penelope's unwavering courage
thwarting suitors & armored adversaries back home.

~ Sterling Warner

ZEBRAS

Safari West, Santa Rosa, California

Time for give and take
Sustenance in black and white
A balanced bonding

~ Dawn Smart

Black and white stripes—both.
Small one reaches under mom.
What guzzling. What love.

~ Carol Park

CAPTIVE MENAGERIE

Equine stripes paint
forms on the horizon
knees lock, ears laid-back
legs long and short stand
erect as a foal suckles
its indulgent mare, downcast
eyes examine the rocky soil
and barren terrain offset
by spindly tree trunks imagine
foraging for leaves and wandering
fields of sweet grass—filly by its side—
liberated from a wildlife refuge.

~ Sterling Warner

Secure the child stands
sheltered in sunlight
sustained by sacred sweetness

~ Cathy Warner

Striped black and white bonds
Mother and child nourished
Holy sustenance!

~ Lisa Sadleir-Hart

NEON MUSHROOMS

Cincinnati Museum of Art

Vibrant fungi sing
Stems aglow, gills pulsate love
What more is there now?

~ Lisa Sadleir-Hart

Ohhhh—psychedelic
Maybe I nibbled too much
Spinning and dancing

~ Dawn Smart

Under mushroom awnings
Alice wanders awestruck
Drinking neon dreams

~ Cathy Warner

DAYGLOW

Lundberg glass nightmare
tangerine & burgundy
mushrooms sprout like trees
on a black marble dais
neon gas rainbows shimmer.

~ Sterling Warner

SPORES

Psychedelic mushrooms
    Tower above scurrying life
Cleaning debris, releasing
    Life nurturing elements
Spread by spore
The magic of
    Regeneration,
The magic of
    Wonder,
The magic of
    Dreams.

~ Carolyn Wiley

DANDELION

Blowing good wishes to the wind
Enabling them to grow again
In another skin.

~ Thom Woodruff

Little fairy seeds
from globe-like mother gust
fly far, seldom close.

~ Carol Park

Parasols of grace
Catch the wind, cast your seeds wide
Take root, grow in light!

~ Lisa Sadleir-Hart

So fragile looking
Yet long-distance travelers
Tougher than they look

~ Dawn Smart

DANDELION

Once yellow as sunshine
Now white as a waning moon.
Gone to seed.
Seeds hold the promise of life;
Each carries a prayer within:
Name them Peace.
One deep breath shatters the globe.
Free fragile filaments
Drift away.
Each seed seeks a new home.
A message of faith
Falls to earth.
The seed
Named Peace
Takes root.
The idea of peace can flourish
In fertile soil, or on fallow ground.
The dream will
Not be extinguished.

~ Carolyn Wiley

Parachuting pappi*
swirl in the wind, carry life
on the wings of a wish

~ Cathy Warner

*the fluff of a dandelion seed; plural

SEATTLE SATELLITE DISHES

ALL OUR EARS ARE EYES

They dropped from round heavens
And are looking up
To find their way home again

~ Thom Woodruff

Are they really there?
Looking down as we look up?
Knowing while we guess.

~ Dawn Smart

PARABOLIC CURVES

Carrier pigeons eye skyscraper
windows, plan aerial gymnastics,
initiate flight patterns & assault glass
walls rooted in concrete, ascending
into the heavens where they pelt
the structure and pedestrians below
with ranch dressing calling cards.

Satellite discs litter TV station roofs
unstable connections abound, blind spots
in the universe drop signals, voices
sound three sheets to the wind, yet they
remain eager to absorb transmissions
like passé feathered messengers jostling
for microwave data in outer space.

~ Sterling Warner

Sonic steel scans the skies
seeking signals to shape and scatter.
Beware the singing sirens.

~ Cathy Warner

Satellite dishes
Signals cross, tangles data
Despair, hope ensues?

~ Lisa Sadleir-Hart

PEREGRINO CAFÉ

near the Sanctuario de Chimayo, New Mexico

PEREGRINO CAFÉ

At the cafe of tres crosses
Ojo de Dios
Sees all
Knows all
Bestows love
On all who enter here
And all who leave
Todos Santos
Vaya con Dios

~ Carolyn Wiley

St Katrina

Katrina lost all
Parents, sight, tribe to pox.
French brought it; plus Christ.

Europeans killed
Tribal villages and souls—
A healer, she held Christ.

~ Carol Park

Cruces arriba
el café de abajo
alma cálida

Crosses above
the coffee below
warm souls

~ Dawn Smart

Thursday at the Pilgrim Café
Jesus pours coffee and soda
Stoops to wash weary feet

~ Cathy Warner

Three crosses stand
Only one resurrects!
And he was double-crossed.

~ Thom Woodruff

RED RHODODENDRONS

Under skies leaden with grief
all that we love blooms, bleeds, dies.
Still we bless hope, its feathers too long in coming.

~ Cathy Warner

A weighted threat looms
Crimson life stands against it
Shedding floret tears

~ Dawn Smart

Rhododendron weeps,
Blood red blossoms surrender
Gracing Gaia's feet.

~ Lisa Sadleir-Hart

CREDO

Mulberry grey marble fills
skies east to west, north to south
backdrop for a maelstrom speeding,
vortex touching down on flowers:
burgundy buds dip beneath
hard rain like infant heads
receiving baptismal showers
then fall at the feet of nature's
altar, christening damp earth
with bloody reverence; fresh blooms
embellish barren branches, recapture
ephemeral blossoms—innocence lost.

~ Sterling Warner

HEADSTONE

Samuel Blackstone, Oak Hill Memorial Park, San Jose, California

Grandparents' tombstones—
their homes and stories long gone.
Too late, I wonder.

~ Carol Park

TOMBSTONE

The stone is weather-worn,
The red granite slab declares
To all who pass this place
The flame of life is gone.

Hill country farm a mile down the road
Was a dreamed-of retirement home
A symbol of an enduring bond
Between him and his wife.

But his essence is not here interred,
His bones rest as relics of time, but
His spirit and soul escaped confinement.
He lives on in the hearts of those who knew him.

That tangible family history ended here.
There have been other sons and other wives
Only this beloved son lies by his mother's side
At the edge of this dying hill country town.

~ Carolyn Wiley

EVEN THE NAMES

on the grave
get washed away
like memory's
waves

~ Thom Woodruff

DEATH

I've been preoccupied with death lately.
At the age where I should have made final plans years ago
It wasn't until my partner's diagnosis of Alzheimer's
That it hit home for me.
The illusion that we have all the time we need
Became we don't have much time left.

So, we've been visiting cemeteries, memorial forests
Online promises of turning our ashes into art pieces–
Garden globes or jewelry.

My favorite so far is a beautiful building
By a famous female architect where rooms filled with light,
Plants and stone, house bookcases of cremains
Enclosed in urns shaped like books.
The rooms wind together creating hours of walking
In contemplation while listening to Musicians playing peacefully.
The place seems alive with activity not just during funerals;
A place for the community to enjoy.

Somehow, I can see myself there
Welcoming the next generation
Who are looking for their final resting place.

~ Gayle Lindsay Slaten

SENTINELS

Lilies, carnations, gladioli rise
from my ashes rather than dust

buried & fermented six feet under
fodder for grub worms and gophers

tunneling beneath the earth's surface
in search of solitude & natural selection

Red breasted robins perch on my headstone
as predators & caretakers, listen to sounds

of silent burrowing, examine dirt, locate
excreted castings & vermi-compost;

beaks aerate moist soil, pecking & plucking
nightcrawlers from my necropolis.

~ Sterling Warner

Pioneers in the family
plot rest untended as memory
cracks like stone.

~ Cathy Warner

STARGAZER LILIES

Easter Sunday

Orchids & Easter Lilies

Burst forth with resurrected effulgence.
How like the moon to be a flower
that is brought forth by the sun.

~ Thom Woodruff

Think on the lilies
buried, lifeless—and then
behold, behold!

~ Cathy Warner

HAWAIIAN BLUES

(or Kokoa's Gentle Surprise)

Before fear of high-jacking terrorists
spread caution, restricting air bridges
& tarmacs to island passengers,
plumeria and purple orchid *Hipu'u*
encircled necks, wrists, & ankles
of provocative grass-skirted women
who'd toss carnation, kika, ginger
lily leis over heads of recent arrivals.

Aloha. Aloha! Aloha! floated from
lips like tropical breezes, followed
by rows of outstretched arms, guiding
hands directed people where to look—
& at whom—cameras clicked, photo ops
flourished, eye expression united fancy
with expectations till wahines dampened spirits
distributing ukulele framed shutterbug cards.

~ Sterling Warner

Vibrant magenta
Bursting with life and green joy
Celebrate the day

~ Dawn Smart

LOST TOY

Children's eyes brighten
cuddling fantastic bunnies.
Rejects heap in dumps.

~ Carol Park

Wedged between here, and?
Straddling an awkward track
Where to go from here?

~ Lisa Sadleir-Hart

Life can be cruel
Easter's adoration
Passing so quickly

~ Dawn Smart

Toy bunny abandoned
like so many childish dreams dropped
from the ladder of years.

~ Cathy Warner

CADBURY RABBIT UNDONE

Grasping a square Kleenex box
the filthy remains of a Peter Rabbit
clutch toy—minus shoes & blue jacket—
hides from moonbeams, avoiding
all gardens, squeezes between steel
girders & iron rivets so tightly his
stuffing explodes over spars, lodging
amongst pillars of strength & open air,
eyes ever watching azure skies above,
safety assured, clinging to existence
secure from white rapids striking nature's
own like a tidal wave of McGregor's rakes.

~ Sterling Warner

SEWING MACHINE

Gilded beauty, yet
industry at the ready
for powerful arms.

~ Dawn Smart

Not one stitch, but nine
to thread the hole ripped by time
and sew it fast to the divine.

~ Cathy Warner

CYLINDRICAL SPOOL

Some claim I have a Singer doppelgänger—please!
My pedigree's incomparable; just call me Jones.

I sit in corners often dark, sometimes bright
gold leaf flowers & vines embellish
my ebony body from horizontal arm
& fiber spindle to vertical regulator;
hardworking seamstresses who dwell
in treadle mysteries, applaud my vintage
hand crank & serpentine neck—extol

black patented curves crafted in British shadows:
Audenshaw factory mass production.

My feed dog pulls fabric, chiffon to denim,
linen to wool, twill to cotton, silk to velvet, as my
vibrating shuttle stimulates arthritic fingers
spinning wheels, guiding cloth, enduring pricks;
a cast iron exhibitionist, I conceal a 4-inch oak drawer
where bobbins mix with needles, straight pins prick thread
spools & tailor's chalk nests with seam rippers.

I want to be used by a novice or couturier—*let me
give you a straight-stitch*—not remain a museum attraction.

~Sterling Warner

SCRAP METAL

Trashed bicycles,
Disgraced water heaters, ranges,
What else will we heap upon Thee, Gaia?

~ Lisa Sadleir-Hart

Piled high and wide
Leftovers of our lives
Weighing down the earth

~ Dawn Smart

RECYCLE

Truth can never be reached by just listening to the voice of authority. –Francis Bacon

Once good ideas
Become stagnant
Lose relevance
Smell like day-old fish.

Truth was relative
Truth could be bought
Truth could be sold
Until truth had no meaning.

In the name of progress,
Land was claimed.
Wealth and power
Guided the leaders.

White invaders came
Conquered, subdued, took
Erasing cultures,
Erasing people.

Take, break, be first
It's the American way.
Harvest, use, discard
It is our right.

With little
Consideration
For the history
Nor respect for the future

Eventually
Killing the land
Fouling the waters
Polluting the air.

~ Carolyn Wiley

Smelted, pounded, purchased, scrapped,
the metal mountain's endless fate
cannot our appetites sate.

~ Cathy Warner

ANTHROPOMORPHIC JUNKYARD

Frigidaires, washers, dryers & sinks
lay side by side, on top, or beneath

water heaters, ovens, bar-b-cue pits
& microwaves—some of them

waste away, relenting a lifetime
without celebrity or a past beyond

energy efficiency—utility taken
for granted unless natural gas lines break

electric coals burn out, or freon pipes
leak; gloved hands load imperfect devices

in truck beds, trailers & trunks— toss them
sans ceremony: brusquely, rudely, callously

smashed by buckets, crushed under backhoe
wheels, picked up and dropped in heaps

that creak as sunlight heats & expands metal
wail as wind passes through hanging glass doors

sheltering rats day & night, providing refuge
from feral dogs & cats always on the chase

untamed creatures appreciative of blazing sky shade
predatory animal protection, a rain & snow sanctuary

before transfer stations load rubble & dispose it out
of sight—at the earth's core—in empty asbestos mines

~ Sterling Warner

EARTH DAY

The earth without art
is "eh," and without earth–void.
We are all weeping.

~ Cathy Warner

Write, paint, sing, dance, plant
Celebrate the earth today
Commit to the fight

~ Dawn Smart

Willow weeps for us,
Her children veered from their home
Of cosmic plenty.

Reflections of tears
Poured mercilessly for Thee
Our great Mother Earth!

~ Lisa Sadleir-Hart

Willow weeps at own reflection
Is this Earth Day?
All my friends are dying!

~ Thom Woodruff

OSIER REFUGE

A weeping willow bows towards a pond—
glassy, still—the tree's image reflects
against cobalt skies, shelters & melts
into nocturnal rites of passage,
aboriginal dreamtime slumber, where I
dwell with ancestral cosmic spirits
neither watching nor guiding human
interactions, just whispering phrases
that linger like relentless earworms, inform
adolescent walkabouts, mid-life appraisals,
elder sagacity—reflections that drift
& settle like fluffy dandelion pappus
as precise as red throated hummingbirds
darting by hibiscus blossoms, drinking
trumpet vine nectar, zig-zagging
over the watery mirror—flurry of wings
buzzing like aging harp strings
beating & exalting willowy freedom.

~ Sterling Warner

WILLOW

In the private sanctuary
Leaning against the
Grey furrowed trunk
Shielded from prying eyes
Behind the willow burka
Free to observe as
The slightest breeze
Moves the trailing boughs

~ Carolyn Wiley

MYSTERY MACHINE

Racing down the road
Drawing stares, raising questions
Mischief here we come

~ Dawn Smart

Psychedelic wheels
Mystical soul journeys
Open the door and begin

~ Lisa Sadleir-Hart

MYSTERY MACHINE

Never trust anyone over thirty. —Jack Weinberg, 1964

The Mystery Machine
Rolls down the road
A throwback to days of yore
Selling…what?
A message of magic
In pink and baby blue.
No draft to protest
No longer at war with war,
But with the threat of war.
Un-won wars continue
Right to water—
Right to breathe—
Right to unionize—
Right to choose—
Right to vote—
All endangered
Inch forward, stumble back.
Antique protesters'
Irate passions subdued
Foregoing psychedelic trips
In a bus adorned in
Day-Glo orange
Neon green,
Eye-scorching pink
Flaming gold
No longer trusting
The under-30 crowd.

~ Carolyn Wiley

EMPTY CHAIRS

Rows of slatted chairs –
I sat, clapped, but now vacate.
Others will applaud.

~ Carol Park

Slatted chairs wait now
Honoring aging milestones
Paying light homage

~ Lisa Sadleir-Hart

Standing straight and tall
We await the performance
Ready for the crowd

~ Dawn Smart

the audience arrives
the experience begins
the joy of jostling elbows

~ Cathy Warner

From Chairman to Chairwoman to Chairperson.
From heteronormative, homosexual to androgynous, transexual.
From uniformity to diversity.
We are more than chairs to sit upon
Even academically, we will not cancel cultures.
Too late to sit (passive) in an audience.
Activate now! Circle up and transform!

~ Thom Woodruff

STEEL BALLET

With fuchsia arms she
reaches–her stretch tall and high–
muscles taut in grace.

~ Carol Park

Seeking salvation
Stretching tall on tippy toes
Reach, you'll make it

~ Dawn Smart

THE DANCER

In memory of Maria Tallchief, Osage Nation, January 24, 1925–April 11, 2013.
First Native American to achieve recognition as a Prima Ballerina and first American
to be recognized in Europe as a Prima Ballerina.

Now stilled,
Confined in mesh
She invaded my life
On a symphonic wave.
An imaginary firebird
Flew across the stage.
The beauty and grace
Of each movement,
Belied the underlying
Strength and skill.
She gave life
To ideas
Translating
Passion into
Fluid movement
Forever enmeshed
In the memory of
A wannabe
Dancer.

~ Carolyn Wiley

CAPITOLA BY THE SEA

Some watch the sky
Some watch the sea
I watch the watchers
Watching me!

~ Thom Woodruff

Bright block bungalows
boisterous and bold
bid sunbathers beachward.

~ Cathy Warner

Colorful cubbies
anticipate with silence
the new day dawning.

~ Dawn Smart

Colors at waterline
Speak of hospitality
Tea with the Divine?

~ Lisa Sadleir-Hart

MALVINA'S HAUNT

Or "Little Boxes" Gone Wild

Malvina Reynolds' ashes once settled
on the bottom of San Francisco Bay
rose to the surface, drawn by an encroaching
presence of 21st century tract homes—
still all made of ticky-tacky; formerly
confined to the Daly City hilltops,
they had extended to sand and surf
like multicolored mold & mildew where
Malvina rested navigating flotsam-jetsam,
finding eternal peace with an undertow
inaccessible to real estate developers
at one with barnacles and mollusks—
even those attached to the BART tunnel—
until recent chips of gaudy rainbow paint
fell from salt weathered walls, drawn
into the bay as high tides reclaim territory
rolling waves sing out a familiar mantra
while Malvina's cremated essence sinks
into watery depths, her protesting whirlpool
gyrating, spinning, sucking, still questioning
"What Have They Done to the Rain?"

~ Sterling Warner

BUNGALOWS

Beach bungalows
Lined up like
Paint swatches
At Home Depot
Reflect the
Captured colors
Of isolated light
Prismatic spectrum
Purloined
Golden orange of sunset
Glowing pinks of sunrise
Cerulean skies
Clouded midway mauve
Aqua oceans
Shimmering violets
Of mollusk nacre
Turn and look
To the sea
And see
The smeared
And blended palette
Mixed by the
Master's unseen hand.

~ Carolyn Wiley

STEALTH SHIP

Navy communications ship, Port Orchard, WA

Stealth ship slips
through Puget Sound's mist.
Shush, don't make a sound.

~ Cathy Warner

Veiled arms afloat
Gray upon gray upon gray
Threat in monotone

~ Dawn Smart

What ship stands by large
as a field in mist, spires, guns?
What looms, captain, near?

~ Carol Park

Ghost ship emerges
On a secret rendezvous
With ancients unknown

~ Lisa Sadleir-Hart

FOG

Dense fog
Enfolds the world
In silvery-lilac light
Tree and shorelines of
Near islands obscured.
In the stillness of slack tide
No breeze ripples
The mirrored surface.
Distant vibrations are felt,
But, not yet heard until
A ghostly cargo vessel
Materializes from the fog
The industrial transport link
Between forest, mill, lumber yard.
Old growth timber no longer
Stands between the wealth of "was"
And the wealth to be gleaned
Fish, fowl, and animal
Face an uncertain future.
The fog bank
Shifts and swirls
And enfolds the world
In the silvery lilac light.

~ Carolyn Wiley

KALALOCH BEACH SUNSET

Saying our goodbyes
To the day, the sea, the sun
Until tomorrow

~Dawn Smart

In coral fire of
sunset, rambling close to shore,
two uphold each other.

~ Carol Park

Light, however dull
Animates all shadow dancers
Joined at the dark

~ Thom Woodruff

ROSE-TINTED PACIFIC

Loving heads bow under magenta skies
bright sun muted behind a long fuchsia veil.

Glancing at tidepools, an arm-in-arm couple
examines shellfish waiting impatiently for high tide.

Temporally land-locked, surfperch commit
saltwater suicide after birthing fingerlings.

Seagulls circle the Pacific shoreline like vultures
scavenging lifeless forms, cleaning up beaches.

Waves roll in a series, cresting highest at seven
reclaiming all sand, puddling under an ice moon.

~ Sterling Warner

Side by side we walk
Conversation rich with love
Mystery and hope

~ Lisa Sadleir-Hart

APRIL SWIRLS

Photo by Michal Lauren

We are bound to fall time, and time again,
Taking us to the great distances,
We create,
To remove ourselves from ourselves,
To seemingly play upon all the uncomfortable stages,
That we construct to be tugged at by our core.

Daily we cross the bridges of our unknown reaches,
We grasp for our personal star to hold our helm steady.
We nurse our desires, especially the one, just out of reach,
Waiting at the windows of our daydreams,
Under the awnings of colorful pretensions,

Wishing upon faery flowers, as we did, as children.
These illusions dance in and out of my radar,
In both waking and sleeping hours.

The Sirens of Desire beckon.
Cafes' lure me to spill ink,
While caffeinated visions amp my inhibitions.
I find myself often under a canopy of grief,
Weeding my personal graveyard,
Measuring all that is buried there.
I keep finding the promise of new blooms
Even in that realm of me so long deserted.

There are lost treasures of myself
And new ones to encourage to grow
To sew these hopeful dreams into the seams
Of my new blue jeans!
No smoke screens please,
I long for what is tangible right now.
I want to remove the scrapheap
Of that which no longer serves…anything.

Return me to my quest into the mysterious.
To engage once again, childlike,
Or as a nymph dancing in a burgeoning rebirth.
Let me place myself into a crayon box of renewed choices.
Let me not stoop to judgement by how I appear,
Move me through the mist of the foggy misperception of beauty.

As much as I revel in the amber light that welcomes the night,
My sun is not ready yet to set.
I shall raise a cup of kindness to myself each dawning day,
As I continue to brew the ever-evolving tastes of me.

~ Michal Lauren

CHEERS!

Cheers to the poet
the poem, the bright words of life!
We drink to delight!

~ Cathy Warner

CONTRIBUTORS

Genét Bosqué—poet, novelist, solo performer—published her first *book Strange Meat: Poems* at 25, is currently editing a chapbook, *Poems of Angst and Incandescence — Pandemic 20/21*, and has been published in numerous literary journals. Most recently, her poem "Women Arise Now ~ Water to Fire," written for International Women's Day, appeared in *Tulip Tree Review – Wild Women* Issue. She feels poetry *must* be spoken to be lived. Genét lives in Chumash land with her pet pterodactyl, Sweetie.

Jan Haag taught journalism, English, and creative writing at Sacramento City College for more than three decades before her retirement in 2021. A former magazine editor, she is the author of *Companion Spirit*, a collection of poems about her husband's death published by Amherst Artists & Writers Press. She leads in-person writing groups in Sacramento, as well as virtual ones. Find her at janishaag.com.

Having earned his MFA from Queens University of Charlotte, **Geoffrey Hall** served as Poetry Editor for the *Rio Review* and as a judge for the Balcones Poetry Prize. His work has appeared in *The Main Street Rag*, *The Ocotillo Review*, and other publications, and has aired on KOOP 91.7 FM, Austin. When he's not hosting online creative writing events, Geoffrey enjoys hiking the Texas Hill Country or playing viola.

It's been said that **Michal Lauren** is a "spiritually enlightened female Johnny Cash of the mystical mountains." Born in Berkeley on the turning tide of the Beat Generation, she makes her home in the redwoods of California's Santa Cruz Mountains. Inspired by pastoral and political poetry, sunsets and mystical imagery, Michal writes to empower and move others into hopeful action. She pulls her audience into a brighter dawn, daring them to dream big.

Lynn Oatman is retired and tries to walk five miles a day, weather permitting. She lives with her feline companion in Liverpool, New York, between the Adirondacks and the St. Lawrence River, too far away from Lake Ontario. She's written poetry since she was a teenager and has been published in *Viral Verse: Poetry of the Pandemic* and *Poemographs*.

Carol Park's homes range from suburbs to wilderness. Six years in Tokyo and Kobe, Japan greatly altered this California girl. Hiking, gardening, mentoring, and reading are her joys. She also enjoys teaching ESL, literary and spiritual community, and the hearth. A multitude of friends from various countries nurture her. Her MFA comes from Seattle Pacific University. Her poetry has been published in *SLANT, Minerva Rising, The Haight Ashbury Journal, MiGoZine, Monterey Review,* and the anthologies *Viral Verse: Poetry of the Pandemic* and *New Contexts:2* and *3.* Her novel nears completion, and her poetry chapbook searches for a home. Find her at CarolPark.us.

Dawna Petersen lives in the Rincon Valley where she spends her time soaking in the beauty of the Sonoran desert and creating an occasional poem or piece of art and encouraging others to do so, too. She is privileged to offer spiritual direction to persons whose souls long to be seen and heard. Before retiring to Arizona, she made and sold ice cream in a quaint shop she owned with her husband in Indiana. She still eats ice cream, but no longer makes it.

Lisa Sadleir-Hart makes her home in Sitka, Alaska. She offers spiritual direction/companionship, and teaches gentle, restorative, and Yasodhara yoga. She and her husband, Tom, own Anam Cara Family Garden & Kitchen, a community supported micro-farm, growing food for fellow Sitkans during the summers. She's an enthusiastic food preserver and can often be found in her kitchen jarring up the jams that are part of her garden-share program. She is also passionate about climate change and advocates on the Divine Mother's behalf with the Citizens Climate Lobby and Transition Sitka. She dabbles in poetry and collage.

Gayle Lindsay Slaten is author of *Self Portraits of A Runaway Wife*, and contributor to *Poemographs,* and *Viral Verse: Poetry of the Pandemic.* Former Poetry Editor for downtownLAlife.com, and a former guest columnist for the *Key Peninsula News* in Washington, she shares her writing to help others know life can change in a moment, just by taking that one step. Gayle is a retired Marriage and Family Therapist and has a teaching credential in Special Education. She recently moved from Tucson, Arizona to Southern California with her partner. Visit her Facebook page: Gayle Lindsay Slaten, Poetry and Prose.

Dawn Hanson Smart is a part-time oyster farmer, hiker, bird watcher, gardener and lover of art, music, and her dog Luna. Dawn has published three novels and has had several poems accepted in competitions and included in other anthologies. She lives in Union, Washington where she grew up and returned to in retirement.

Cathy Warner is author of two volumes of poetry: *Home By Another Road* and *Burnt Offerings*; and editor of three poetry anthologies: *Poemographs for Peace, Poemographs,* and *Viral Verse: Poetry of the Pandemic.* She lives on the shores of Washington's Hood Canal near the Skokomish River estuary where she writes short fiction, essays, and poetry, renovates homes, and photographs wildlife, the landscape, and the night sky. Her writing has appeared in dozens of literary journals in print and online. Find her at cathywarner.com.

An award-winning author, poet, and former Evergreen Valley College English Professor, **Sterling Warner's** works have appeared in many literary magazines, journals, and anthologies including *Danse Macabre, Otoliths: A Magazine of Many E-Things, Anti-Heroin Chic, Unlikely Stories, Mark V, Lothlórien Poetry Journal, Ekphrastic Review,* and *Sparks of Calliope.* Warner's collections of poetry include *Rags and Feathers, Without Wheels, ShadowCat, Edges, Memento Mori: A Chapbook Redux, Serpent's Tooth,* and *Flytraps* (2022)—as well as *Masques: Flash Fiction & Short Stories.* Currently, Warner writes, hosts/participates in virtual poetry readings, turns wood, and enjoys retirement in Union, Washington.

Linda Whaley finds peace in God's word and his creation. She explores writing styles without a map. Her muse is amused, footloose, and reckless at times; reclusive, thoughtful, and probing at others. She loves ellipses, is bemused by commas, and often runs out of exclamation points!!! If you know of a miniature elephant that will not grow larger than a Labrador, please contact her forthwith. Check out her fiction book, *Those Before Never Leave.*

Award winning humorist and native Texan, **Carolyn Wiley**, watches the morning sun light up the icy slopes of Mt. Rainier from her perch on a South Puget Sound bluff. When not responding to Cathy Warner's photo/poetry challenges, or writing grants for community causes, this retired educator advocates for arts, digs in the dirt, designs quilts, makes jewelry, teaches tai chi sword fighting, and explains how the world works to fans of her *Key Peninsula News* column "Devil's Head Diary."

Sprit Thom, aka **Thom Woodruff**, is an improvising bard who works best with musicians. He toured with Mother Gong and is the 2020–2022 Beat Poet Laureate of Texas.

Made in the USA
Columbia, SC
09 January 2023

75027897R00095